Beginners Guide to Genealogy:

Uncover Your Family's Secret History

Elaine Hodgkinson

Beginners Guide to Genealogy

About 'Beginners Guide to Genealogy'

Published In the United Kingdom by
Hodgkinson Publishing Limited

© Copyright Hodgkinson Publishing Ltd
2010 All Rights Reserved

Online: HodgkinsonPublishing.com

Table Of Contents

Introduction

Your family's history is part of your history too. Perhaps learning more about your family will inspire you to be a different person today. Or, perhaps your quest will help open the door to questions that you may have. For others, a quest into their family ancestry is one that will provide them with the tools to pass down information to their own children and then their grandchildren as well. Genealogy is something to strive for.

The quest to learn more about your family is something that people have wanted to know and learn for hundreds of years. The need to know about who, what, where, and when is powerful and virtually any person can relate to wanting more information about their past, whether it's their own or their ancestors.

Our quest to learning your genealogy is a long one and it will take some work. There's nothing simple or easy about the process of unearthing years of history. Yet, the reward that will come from it is a reward that will fulfill your history craving for knowledge. Use this book to help you to begin your quest.

Why You Need To Explore Your Past

It seems simple to understand why history is important. There are countless times that history repeats itself. We are face with the same choices that we were just a handful of years ago. Did we learn from our mistakes or will we make the same ones over and over again?

Whether you believe in a Higher Power or not, there is still the question of what could have happened to those that are in your past. After all, don't you want to know who was in your family tree?

Could you be the descendant of one of the Kings or Queens of England? Perhaps you have an ancestor that was a war hero in the Revolutionary War. Perhaps the past isn't as pretty with ancestors that died in famines, illnesses or strife, only to save their children that you would eventually be descended from.

The "what if" type questions are out there and people in general are curious about what it means for them. If you want to know what your chances of learning more about your past you have to give genealogy a chance. You have to try to learn more.

The good news is that it's quite possible for many people to learn more about those in their family trees. The quest starts with understanding the process of genealogy and then learning how to get started on your own journey to learn as much as you can about those that have come before you in your family tree.

Defining Genealogy

Genealogy is the study of family ancestry. It is the study and tracing of the family's pedigrees. During the process of genealogy, you will collect the names of your relatives, including those that are deceased and will then establish their relationship to each other.

This will include exploring various levels of your family tree as well including primary and secondary family members. You will use both documentation and word of mouth to help you to develop your family tree. The goal is to ultimately build a family tree that includes all of your relatives as far back as you would like to take it, or at least as far as you can take it.

Getting a family history of your family is a bit different. In genealogy, you technically only will get the names of your family members, creating a tree.

But, with a family history, you will take this one step farther by including information about each of those people. Learning more about the lives they lived is part of getting your family history.

Sometimes, this can be done at the same time as creating a family tree, other times it is a bit more complex because of how difficult it can be to learn this information. The goal is to gather as much information about your ancestors as you can to better understand your family's history in both public and private life.

The Genealogist

One of the many people that you may find at your side during the process of understanding your family history is that of your genealogist. A Genealogist is someone that does the work of genealogy, rather he or she collects the data that is later used to piece together family trees and family histories.

If you use a professional genealogist to track your family's history, you will hire them to do several key things for you. They will work to uncover your past.

Their job is to get as many oral histories and preserve your family's history as much as possible. They do this first through living relatives that you have. Then, they push through various tools to gain information on your ancestors, those that are no longer alive.

The genealogist works to understand as much as possible about those that they are uncovering. This often means more than just knowing their names, but also learning about their lifestyle, their motivations in their lives and even piecing together a biography for the family.

The benefit of using a genealogist for your study of your own family tress is that they have experience (or should at least!) in the process. This means that they have the necessary information to work through old laws, political boundaries that were once in place, immigration trends and historical information to find the answers to your family tree's questions.

Yet, you don't have to use a genealogist for your journey into your family's past. You can gain information about your family in a number of ways. While it may be easier for you to hand over your family's information and let someone else do the work, this can be costly.

There is also the need for doing your own exploring of information about your family. Many people go through the journey through learning about their family by exploring the details that are out there, gathering facts and understanding the lives that these people lived. That unique experience of uncovering information and learning from your ancestor's past is one journey you may want to do on your own.

The good news is that there is a lot of help for those that are considering a search through their family history available right on the web. You don't have to go through the process on your own and ending up hitting a dead-end that makes you give up.

You can use a number of excellent tools that are available to you on the web. It is completely up to you to determine the right road to take through the process of uncovering your family tree. In fact, in later chapters we'll talk about tools of software that you can use too.

But, we'll assume here that you do want to do this journey on your own or you want further information. For that, let's explore the process of genealogy.

Genealogy And The Search For Answers

The search for information about your family will be a process. It definitely won't happen overnight and it definitely will take some time and research. But, that's the fun part.

There are many ways that you can explore your family's history through the use of the web and various other services that are available to you. Some may work, others will not. Often searching for your ancestry is a process of hit or miss. But, we'll give you many resources to help you on your journey.

Genealogy and History

One important thing to consider is the fact that your ancestry is part of history. Even if you can't get through the search for your family as thoroughly as you would like to, chances are you will learn a great deal about history and the role that your family may have played in that history. It could be small but it could be something important or something significant.

Sometimes, a search for your family's relatives can lead to reunions, or meetings with others that you may not have known or haven't seen in years. When you explore this path, you may find that distant cousins can offer you information. Or, you may find that a fight in the family has lead to a certain area of your family being cut off from you, and it may help to bring you all back together.

In addition to this, you may find that your family was separated for reasons that could not be controlled by them. For example, perhaps a war caused your family to split up.

Or, foster home and adoption may have pushed your family into various directions that you didn't know about.

The fact is; there are likely to be family secrets, hush hush memories and much more that you can uncover when you use genealogy as your tool to uncovering your family's history and behaviors.

Indeed, you are likely to bring your family closer together and to have a better understanding for each other. And, for many people this means piecing back together family traditions and revealing family secrets that should have been told long ago.

Its Role in History

As we mentioned before, in family genealogy, there is a need to know more.

Genealogy is actually something that people have done for centuries, if not longer. The need to know about your past is a natural, human curiosity and for that there have been numerous different people that have strived to learn as much as they can about their past throughout history.

Generally speaking, though, genealogy was something that was only done in olden times for those that were of power. For example, it was important to trace the genealogy of nobles, kings, queens and emperors. Any ruler needed to have information that showed that he was the right ruler for the job. Genealogy was used to help determine who the righteous ruler in many cases was.

If you wanted to claim that you had the right to have wealth and power, then you had to show that your ancestry proved that you were worth it. Demonstrating that you were the rightful heir or the rightful ruler was no little task and only genealogy could make this happen.

On a side note, the coat of arms of a family in the times of royalty where often used to help determine family lineage. This is actually called heraldry. It is the ancestry of royalty that was used in the quartering of the coat of arms of a family.

In many cases, though, modern ancestry studies have shown that many of those that used these methods to "claim" their righteous place in royalty where actually not authentic. They were merely fabrications that didn't prove anything, really.

The most notable of these, of course, are those kings, emperors or other rulers that used their ancestry to show how they were linked to gods and the founders of the civilization itself.

The fact is that genealogy is something that can only be traced through truth, and that is something that is in the eye of the beholder. While you can probably find documentation to support more modern claims of ancestry, going back quite far in time is difficult.

Nevertheless, it is a story that you can tell! Imagine begin able to say that your great, great, great grandfather was part of the Royal Family!

The search for answers, then, will start with the need for authentic answers. For that, we turn to modern methods of uncovering the truth of families, first.

Modern Methods Of Researching Your Past

As we mentioned, learning from facts is one of the best tools that you have in genealogy searches. We'll start with the most basic of searches, the ones that lead you to the answers that you are seeking from the very basic level.

While modern technology and modern research methods are effective, we'll also explore some of the lesser beneficial methods of genealogy research which can actually be helpful to connect the dots.

The Advent of Change

While most people have always been interested in genealogy, it was always something on the backburner, so to speak.

Yet, there was something that happened in the 1970's that made genealogy come to the forefront and began our search for more answers as well as the ability to us modern research methods to tackle them.

Of course, that was the television adaptation of *Roots: The Saga of an American Family.* This was a fictionalized account of Alex Haley's family history.

It was the beginning of people questioning what their family's history had in store for them. Could you have some powerful past that you didn't know about? This television program really sparked the questions that people had and they began the search for information which would grow into a steady habit for many years.

Today's interest in the past is fueled by many sources. Before going any farther, though, we must provide you with a word of warning. The fact is that the internet is one of the best tools that you have to connecting you with your long lost family and giving you answers to questions about who your relatives were.

Yet, it is also an easy way for you to find yourself in a trap. Sometimes, information that you find is not going to be accurate. This is especially true of those methods found on the web that can't be proven accurate. Nevertheless, there are ways that you can connect the dots and learn quite a bit about your family's past.

The process often consists of looking in unique areas, often ones that you haven't thought of or realized that your family may possibly be a part of it. Uncovering your family's history means going deep into the process.

Research Effort Methods

The process of learning about your family is likely to be one that offers several key searches. You'll use a wide range of these methods to get to the answers you need.

- Types of relationships among your family members will include kinship to various groups or associations.

- A surname search is called a one name study which will only give you details about a certain family name, passed down over time.

- A small community, village or even church parish may offer help in the research methods. This also includes a one place study, which is just a search of on location's family lines.

- Or, you can use a particular person to search for, for example trying to use your family's history to connect to another person's family.

The truth is that you'll likely need to go through many of these methods to find the answers that you need. In many ways, it's a process of looking where you didn't know you needed to look for answers regarding your family.

Latter Day Saints

Don't skip over this section just yet! Even if your family doesn't have any known connection to the Church of Jesus Christ of Latter Day Saints, commonly known as LDS, you may still be able to use their records to help you to learn about your family.

During the 1900's, this group worked hard to create a program of moving all of their available records on ancestry into the valuable tool of microfilm. They placed all records they had in this medium, to safeguard them. In addition to this, they also created an index that was used to keep track of all of their members.

These two undertakings were large, thorough and would become one of the best tools for genealogical searches today. Today, these two projects have been folded together and are in two databases that are readily accessible.

The International Genealogical Index, which is known as IGI, is a tool that can be used. It is a transcription record of filmed civil and ecclesiastic records. These records have come from various locations from cooperating local areas around the world.

The other database that you can use is known as the Ancestral File or just simply AF. This database is used to collect the information about the member's contributions over time.

So, how can these databases help you? First off, the IGI is one of the best records of old birth and marriage records from the LDS. It has records of those that have been born, died and married starting from well back to 1500. Most of this information is from the United States, Europe and Canada.

Generally, information regarding members has been able to reveal quite a bit about family ancestry from these resources.

How can you use the LDS's collection of information? In Salt Lake City, Utah the collection of these microfilms is located. The resources are located at the Family History Library which has a vast collection of information regarding the entire society.

Yet, you don't have to travel there to find them. There are branches (some 4000 of them) around the country and world that can offer you help.

You can visit these locations, request information or even rent information for your on-site research needs. In fact, they have expanded this search ability to the internet as well. You can visit the collection at this location at FamilySearch.org.

The website actually provides for free research guide and a variety tools including the Ancestral File, the International Genealogical Index, the Social Security Death Index, and the 1880 United States Federal Census information. This is an ideal place for you to get started with your search!

Use Your Genetics for Genealogy

What if you could have your DNA tested at a local lab and then reported to you. It could be then used to trace your family line, based on your DNA well back into history.

How can this be possible when DNA is something that is rather new? The fact is that today, DNA is adding to the genealogical search quite a bit. Those that are studying genealogy are finding that this is a great way to actually learn about your past. But, how does DNA and genealogy work together?

There are two types of DNA that are important to be considered for genealogy purposes. The first is mitochondrial DNA which is the type of genetic marker that is passed down by everyone.

Mitochondrial DNA is passed down through the maternal, or female, line. As it is passed down, even through thousands of years, it changes very little. Only small mutations are seen in this type of DNA and that makes it a significant role player in history research.

The other type of DNA which is important is known as Y Chromosome DNA. This type of DNA is only found in males; whereas Mitochondrial DNA is found in everyone. In Y Chromosome DNA, there are only small mutations percent over time in the male lineage. This too makes it very important for the search for family lines.

As you can imagine (soap operas here don't count) the need to know if you are related to someone is done by taking DNA samples of two people and comparing them. By using a genetic test, researchers can see if two people have the right DNA to be related based on these two types we've mentioned.

In genealogy, this happens to be an ideal method for matching people today that may be descendants of others from the past. For example, by taking two people that share a potential common ancestor, tests can help to place where people are in the scope of ancestry.

One study that you may want to look into, then, is that of the Molecular Genealogy Research Project. The MGRP, as it is called, is a database collection of information that is taking genealogical information and genetic data and working to place people throughout the world.

The goal of this project is to establish the fact that everyone is related to everyone else, and then to define just how closely they are related. By taking blood samples and pedigree charts that he had collected, Mr. James L Sorenson, the founder of the project, began to learn as much as he could about how closely related people actually were.

By comparing the data of those that would donate blood samples, this project showed that people were in fact related, though distantly, through generations. You can learn more about this project, and even participate in it by visiting their website.

Another project that should be noted is that of The Genographic Project. This project is one that used genetic methods to actually trace the human patterns of migration and then to determine the biogeographical and ethnic origin. In this project, the results help to place people in various ancestral groups even through some ancient times. It can help to tell you where your ancient ancestors may have lived and experienced.

The fact is that DNA is an ideal tool to use in determining the relation of people. In our search for answers about your own family, though, it may be harder to actually see how DNA can play a role. Nevertheless, it is one of the most amazing types of research methods available and definitely one that will see improvements over time.

These methods of understanding ancestry and genealogy are good places to start. They are tools that could be effective at helping to answer some of your own questions. But, by far they aren't all that you can get into.

The goal of any type of ancestry project is to trace back from the beginning, or rather from the now into the past. Therefore, to get you started in the process of learning about your past, we'll go back and offer you the first steps of understanding your family tree.

In the next chapter, we'll talk about how you can get started in the exploration of your family tree and family history.

Start with the understanding that there are modern means of research available to you, though. You can then use the information that you uncover there to give you the answers that you need.

Where You Need To Start Your Journey

To start your own genealogy project, you do need to start at the beginning, which means getting out some paper and pencils (not pens, because information is likely to change as you go!) and to start talking to your family about what they may be able to tell you.

Your first stop should be those that are older than you, the older the better. Start with parents, your grandparents, your uncles and your aunts. Anyone that's in your family's line is an ideal person to start your research with.

Here are some of the most important pieces of information to gather.

- List their name, including any maiden names they may have.

- List their date of birth and the location of their birth, especially the city

- Question about their youth, where did they grow up, what type of life they lived, what religious organizations they were part of.

- Who were their parents? What information about their parents can they provide to you? This should include information about where and when the parents were married, grew up or anything additional that they can tell you.

- When was the individual you are talking to married? Where were they married?

- Where did their parents meet? Where did their parents work, live and do the things that they did?

- Locations of parent's burial sites can be helpful as well. When they died, where they were buried including the cemetery name if available is important.

- Who was their family growing up? Did they have aunts, uncles, cousins, distant family members that they remember? Gather the same information for these individuals as well.

- Are there family members that are living close by them?

- Are there family members that are buried at the same cemetery as relatives? If so, were and what were their names?

- Ask about their living relatives and the deceased relatives. Is there anyone in the family still alive that's a generation above them that you can talk to? If so, how can you reach them?

Asking these questions is just the start, but a powerful one. You want to open up the lines of communication between you and those that you have alive and available to you. One of the best ways to do this is to use stories.

The Benefit of Stories

Although facts are an important part of the process of learning about those that are in your ancestral line, it's also important for you to consider the stories that these people can tell you, too.

Stories can do quite a bit for you. Obviously, they are important to note for your own understanding of who these people were that are in your family lines. If a person is someone that your grandmother remembers, she can tell you lots of stories about growing up with them.

This allows you to get to know these individuals and really to learn who they were. That's important for creating a family history that offers you a real in depth look at the people, their personalities and their characteristics. In effect, it brings these people back to life for you.

But, stories can do much more for you as well. Let's say that your grandmother starts to talk about her cousin Sue that she grew up with. You don't know Sue so this is something that you want to hear about.

As you listen to her talk about Sue, you learn details about where Sue moved, who she married, where she went after she was married and even children that she may have had.

This means that you now have a more complete family history and family tree that are available to you. You can now pursue Sue or her descendants and get another branch of your tree growing.

Stories can make all of these important facts come to life, which is something that you need. While this is just one example of how they can be beneficial to you, imagine what can happen when you start talking to many people and how their stories can add up to very detailed people.

On the other hand, if you walked up to your grandmother and simple asked her about her family tree, she may mention Sue but that's about all she may remember. But, opening up memories is a great way to learn about your family tree in much more detail and with many more benefits through the process as well.

It's important to talk to as many people as you can that are still alive. The fact is that these people are sources of information that you can then use to help propel you throughout your journey. This is the easy stuff, the information that is readily available. Take full advantage of this information as it will be the easiest to get.

It's important to record the information that is provided to you as well. Even if you are taking written notes, you may be able to go back to your recordings and hear another clue or detail that you missed. Or, you may be able to use this information later for other information that you uncover although right now it may not seem important.

Keep lots of tapes and a recording device available to you to make the process as smooth as possible. Keep these items safe, throughout the process, too.

Creating a Family Tree

Now that you have this information, the next step is putting it in its place. This may be one of the more complicated processes that you have to go through, but it's going to be fun, too.

You have two options. First off, you can use just paper and your notes to create your family tree, which will look like a tree with all of its branches. But, this is hard to keep organized and can be a good tool if it is used correctly and managed.

The other option that you have is Family Tree Software products which can help you to determine an effective, electronic method of managing your family tree. In a later chapter we will talk more about how software can aid you in the process of uncovering your family tree. It's important, though to consider it as a tool for organization if not for finding your family members.

Placing the names of those people that you have learned about on your family tree is a process that requires a good eraser. It will be fun to put the pieces together, but it will also be difficult to organize.

Tips for Managing Your Family Tree

These tips will help you to get your family tree up and running. Your goal is to do the best that you can to keep it organized, so that it is easy for you to use later.

- Group each person by the family that they belong to. If they have more than one connection, place these families near each other, and show their relation.

- Group families by how they are related. If the two men are brothers, note this. Determine how each family relates to each other and note it.

- Sometimes, using index cards can help you to keep large families organized. Even for those that are alive, create an immediate family index card, which includes the family, members, dates of birth and location that you can refer to later, over and over again.

- Place blank spots near those people that you haven't found. For example, if you find out that there's a sister to one of your cousins that you don't know their name, mark that there is a sister. Later you may find their name and information.

Every once in a while, go back to the beginning of the project and see if there are any blanks that you can fill in. Often, you can learn a lot without realizing it.

It also pays to include others in this information that you've found. For example, if you are working on your genealogy project with your sister or aunt, when they see your family tree laid out, they may remember some additional information from the information that you have gathered. This information is important to gather.

The Importance of Pictures

Another path that you should go down with each of the people that you talk with is that of pictures. While you may not have a lot of photos yourself of your past generations, you probably have pictures of your parents and your grandparents that are treasured by you. You would never give up those pictures because they hold memories for you and the same holds true for others.

Let's say that as you are talking to your mother about her family tree she realizes that she has some photos of her childhood and perhaps you would like to look at them? By doing this it can help you to ask questions and even learn more.

While looking at the photos you may find a picture of someone you don't know. A question gets you an answer and the end result is another name is filled in on your chart!

In addition to gathering people's names and information, a genealogy project can also be benefited by having other information from the photos. You can learn what they are doing in the picture, where it was taken, perhaps what school it was from and even information about the ages of people in relation to others.

This information is easy to benefit from in a genealogy search. Make sure that you talk to every person that you have in your family about the photos that they may have. Or, even ask if their parents had photos that may be tucked away some place that you could look at. Even without firsthand accounts from the people in your family they can help you. A simple note on the back of the photo provides great information to you.

Photos are also prized possessions to use in creating your family tree, too. For example you can easily place these on your documentation to make names come to life.

The fact is that it's essential for you to actually learn as much as you can through this process from those that are still alive.

The Records Search Begins Now

Now that you have a basic understanding of what's happening with your family at least to the level that they remember, you can begin your records search. The goal of this step is to help reinforce what you have learned from them and through that learn more.

There are many ways that you can make this happen, though. It's not necessarily a difficult process. We'll go through a number of different methods that you can use to actually pull this information in.

How Records Came To Be

As we mentioned before, many of the method and understandings of ancestry started with the methods that were used by royalty and other rulers. The method of recording things, though, didn't stay just with nobility for very long.

By the 16th century, much of Europe was beginning to record their lives through records. To keep track of their citizens, countries began to take records into account.

These records were more than just birth and death certificates, though. The included things like marriage licenses, documentations for anything that were important during their life helped to create a paper trail.

If they needed a permit for something, needed to file some type of report or had a major life change happen, it generally was recorded on paper somewhere.

During this time, most of these records were kept in their local and regional offices but also national offices or archives were used to keep track of everything that could be kept track of during this time.

Now, why does this matter to you? As you begin your records search, you should know how a genealogist undercover answers to their questions. And, often, these answers need to come from the information that has been stored in these ancient records.

Information in these records can be extracted but it can be difficult to get your hands on them without some type of genealogical experiment. Nevertheless, they are an ideal way to learn how families are connected and how relationships grew. Even more so, they are used to help create family trees and timelines which you can still use today.

The Records Search Begins

Where does your records search begin? Like how European and later other areas did, most of the United States has records that can be tapped into from various regions.

As part of your search for answers about your own family, you need to tap into the paper trail that's in place. From current families to those that lived years ago, there is likely to be some form of paper trail that you can use.

Here are some of the paper items that you should consider looking at for each of the people in your family tree, even those that you think you know enough about.

Birth Certificates

The birth certificates of those in your family tell a wealth of information. Birth certificates are a good way to find out everything that you need to know about a person and their history.

You can find out what hospital they were born in, the name of the mother and father. Most birth certificates of the past give the name of the father as well as the mother. It was considered a shame, at one time, to have no father on the birth certificate as a child was labeled "illegitimate." As this was the case, most mothers did their best to get the name of the father printed on the birth certificate.

The age of the parents is usually on there and perhaps the county where they were born.

Like death certificates, birth certificates are recorded in the county where the birth took place. Many people hit a dead end here because their relatives were born in another country.

Death Certificates.

Death Certificates can be obtained from the county in which the person died. It is the law that a death certificate must be recorded and made part of public records.

If you know the county where the person died and the date that they died (as well as their name and social security number - which you can get from the social security records) you can write to the county and ask them for a copy of their death certificate. You will probably have to pay a few dollars for them to copy it for you. You do not need a certified copy of the certificate, which usually costs more than double. You just need a copy.

Once you get the copy of the death certificate, you will find the following information:

- Place of death
- Place of birth
- Attending physician (the person who signed the death certificate)
- Birth date
- Name of spouse
- Name of parents (if known at the time)
- Date of marriage
- Area last residing
- Cause of death (this is being eliminated from death certificates in recent years due to privacy factors)

Once you have this information, you have more pieces to your puzzle that can be put together. The information that is put on the death certificate varies depending on the person who died and the circumstances. Not all of them carry the name of the parents.

Marriage and Divorce Records

Marriage and divorce certificates are like any other public record. In fact, unless a divorce is sealed, you can find out petitions for divorce and why the petitioner sought the divorce. Anything that goes through the court is public record

Baptism Records

They connect you with godparents, religious organizations and more.

Adoption records

These can be had for those over the age of 18. But, some family members may be able to provide you with additional information regarding them if they happened.

Census records

Cemetery records or, possibly, funeral homes and tombstone records.

City Records

Some are even available on the web. Others you'll need to visit city hall to learn more about first.

Criminal Records

These can help to form connections and to tell stories about your family members.

In these records listed, you can see where you'll find information that can easily be used to track your family. For example, in birth records, you can easily go through the process of learning parents, relations that may be listed, addresses and even where the child was born.

In other records, such as in divorce records, this can show where the family was headed. Did you lose a branch of your family when great grandparents divorced?

Look at these following record search options to determine if your family could have filed them.

Sometimes, just searching for these records for known family names can help to pull up a bunch of different pieces of information that you can later use to fulfill your needs in creating a family tree. Of course, you'll learn about those people at the same time as well.

- Biographies, or biographical profiles, Consider Who's Who, for example

- Coroner's reports, if available, can help you to learn more about how people died.

- Diaries, if you can find them, will help you to establish answers to your questions. If the person is deceased, these are easy to benefit from without stepping on anyone's toes. In addition, read through the personal letters, cards or even family Bibles that may be in people's personal effects.

- Telephone directories of the locations that your family lived can be helpful, especially if you know where your family members lived.

- Newspapers, many of which can be found at your local library are a source of information that you must take into account. These can help provide you with search abilities too.

- Photographs, as we have discussed should also be used. They can help jog memories. Many families had family portraits down which can easily show you who are in the family, even those that may have left the family or died, too.

- Medical records, if obtainable, can be a useful tool as they often listed family members on them as well as locations.

- Occupational records can be a paper trail to consider. If you knew where someone worked, you may find additional information about them there as well, including past employment that they had before that location and where they moved to or from.

All of these records can be used for their each individual benefit. By asking questions to your family about these records and finding out what's available, you could uncover even more information than you thought you had available to you.

Social Security Records

You can use an online website to dig up social security records or you can go to www.socialsecurity.gov to find out about the registry. You will probably have a better time looking up the records at an online site than you will through the social security administration.

If you are not sure about the day of death for a relative, or if there are many people who have the same name who died around the same time that your relative died, this is where it gets confusing. You have to go into the records to find out more information about them. This can help you narrow down your search and prevent you from chasing after the wrong leads.

Glean as much information from the social security records as possible. They may have information such as spouse name, birth date and other information. Social security records only go back as far as the 1930s, at which time when social security was adopted. Anyone who died before the 1930s will be difficult to find from these records. But that does not mean that you cannot find them. There are many other public records that the social security records can lead you to after you have located your starter relative on them.

Social security records are easy to find and can be discovered for free for any deceased individual. You cannot get social security records for living persons for obvious reasons

Land Searches

Another important part of the process of learning about ancestors is tapping into the wealth of information available to you through land searches.

People have always owned property. A piece of land was an incredibly important part of life. Even well before people established the United States; land was a mark of nobility, of power and of self accomplishment.

In many ways, the American Dream of owning a house and land was established years before in many other countries around the world. It just came to be more readily in the United States.

Therefore, land records are some of the very best tools that you have available to you to help uncover your genealogical line. Here are some of the records you need to take into consideration:

- Land records from countries, cities and even national records. These show who owned the property, according to official reports and documents. They can be tracked through your auditor's office or other land record office locally.

- Deeds. Deeds are often filed as public records and kept indefinitely.

- Voter registration can also be helpful. These can be found through the same government offices.

- Probate records. When a person dies, their estate often goes through probate, which is how the property is then passed down or confiscated through other means. These records are also public records available through local government offices.

- Wills, which are filed publicly in most cases, can also show how people related, where property and other possessions went after someone died. It can help to connect the dots.

- Tax records. Who doesn't pay tax? Tax records can be helpful to your family search because of the information they provide including property ownership and property location.

School Records

School records can also play a role in the establishment of family trees. In some cases, records have been kept by schools for hundreds of years, which means that if you know which schools your family members attended, you can learn more about them.

If you don't know which schools were used, you can still use the records of local schools to get an idea.

- School records can be searched.

- Alumni records can also be found and searched for information. These can often tell you where people went after they graduated from the school as well.

- Yearbooks and other school photos can be used to help track people.

If you are unsure where family members when to school, your search should take you into the direction of schools in the area in which you know they lived. Don't forget about colleges, because some families did have the ability to send their children to colleges, even though children may not have graduated from there.

Military Records

Military information is not difficult to get. Military records are usually immaculate and will give you the information about your relatives, where they served, if they died in combat, when they were discharged from the service, which branch of the service in which they served and if they were decorated with any medals. Military information contains photographs of those who were in the service.

The VA will also send you medals of your family members who have died and who earned medals during the war. Anyone who has a relative who was in the service can obtain information about them through this route.

Military information should not be overlooked as they have the best records available and date back to the Civil War. You cannot get photos, usually, of those who battled in the Civil War, but you can obtain information about them. Prior to the Civil War, it can be difficult to trace your ancestors as many records were destroyed or lost.

Do not overlook military records if you are searching for family who served in the armed forces. You can go to the Veteran's Administration to get this information. You can even call them and they will be able to direct you to where you need to be.

Other Records to Search

There are still other records that you may not have considered that need to be taken into consideration. Here are some additional records that you need to take into consideration.

- Obituaries. These are often listed and filed in local libraries or through governmental offices.

- Pension plans and records of them can help to provide locations of where payments were sent, family names and information, including beneficiary information such as children or others that funds went to after the person died.

- Passports, these can be found and used to track travel as well as addresses

- Poorhouse, almshouse, workhorse and asylum records. Although you may not think that your family used these, which are generally locations that people went when they no longer could support themselves, they are very often hidden secrets. Records can point you into various directions.

All of these locations are important records to check. Even if you think that your family didn't use these locations, it still can help you to connect the dots and answers questions that may be unanswered.

Because there are so many different records

for you to keep track of, here's a tip to help you to organize the information that you find.

Remember that we told you to make family cards that can help you to keep track of each family and how each of them related to each other? Now, create an index card (usually larger ones work better) that has one person on it. List their information on it.

Include any information that you can about each individual person. This will help you to organize their individual histories as well as their families later. Refer back to those cards often so that you can possibly see where people connected, moved, changes or began relationships with each other.

Of course, if you are using a computer program, this information can be easily tracked on these programs, assuming that they allow for it.

How Did They Get Here?

If you live in the United States or Canada, then your family members probably migrated to these locations at some point from various other countries.

If your family has a heritage that they are proud of and often talk about, this is easy to understand. If your family is a direct descendant of someone that "came over on the boat" then you know that they came from another country usually to seek out the American Dream.

But, where did they come from?

This opens the door from many different questions that you have. If you consider yourself Italian, you believe that your family came from Italy, but could it be Sicily? Or, perhaps it was Northern Italy? If your family is Irish, then you assume that you can from Ireland; but, where in Ireland?

Sometimes, countries don't stay the same as they are today.   Many countries have merged, changed hands and even worse been taken over by other countries. Is this possible for your family?

For example, if your family says that their heritage is German, it could be Hungarian, or others smaller countries in the region in which there was constant land changing hands. By doing a bit of history education can help you to find the answers to your questions regarding where you came from.

How to Begin Your Search

To connect your family to that of those from around the world, you need to search through a number of regions, records and oral histories.

For starters, you need to get stories straight. Depending on how many generations ago your family came to the United States will help to determine just where you should start.

Did your father or mother come to the United States from another country? Did your grandparents? Did your great grandparents? How many generations back did your family members come from another country to settle in the United States or Canada?

Also, remember that your entire family probably did not come over at the same time. Many families had one or two relatives that traveled to North America and settled here. After talking to their left behind relatives, they convinced them that life was great and that they too should come. Then, many additional relatives may have come.

Your aunts, uncles, your grandparent's siblings and so on could have traveled to North America at different times and that's information that you need.

Learning Where They Came From

Through the use of oral histories as well as family histories that you have already learned, you can begin to understand the location that your family came from.

As much as possible, you want to find out where they were coming from. For example, knowing that your family traveled from England to the United States is okay, but you should know from what region of England

and even better what city they came from. This will provide you with more details and give you a definite direction in which you should look for more information.

Do this for all of your relatives, as much as possible, because families don't always live in the same areas.

For example, let's say that your great grandmother came from Venice in Italy. But, her sister may have come from another region. The question is, did your great grandmother's parents live near her or did they live near her sister?

While that sounds confusing the fact is that it's important for you to keep the path of communication moving smoothly so that you can learn as much as possible about your family's history and family tree.

It can be helpful to actually get out a map and talk about it with those that are around too. For example, a map of Italy may help your grandmother to remember that she had cousins in a neighboring city by jogging their memory. Any time you can get any information from those that are around you, it's a plus to do so.

Life Where They Lived

Finally, if you have the ability to do so, check with the local authorities (if possible) to find out even more information. You can find information regarding where they lived, what property records were in place there as well as any other public records that were available.

Take another look at the list of public records in the previous chapter. Can you fill in any of those blanks for your ancestors that came from European or other countries through those types of searches?

Perhaps you can learn about your family's past through a records search of death and birth certificates in the country they came from. To get this information, you may need to know someone in that region or perhaps travel there. Sometimes you'll be able to get the information through a phone call to the city government offices and with a bit of luck.

Gather as much information using those public record searches as you can from your ancestor's home countries. This information can be harder to obtain, definitely, but it's the best tool available to take you back as far as possible into your family's past.

How Did They Get Here?

Once you have learned all that you can about where your ancestors lived, there's still the need to piece together information about them when they arrived in the United States, Canada or even other regions (such as South America.)

To get started, find out what means they used to get here. While to some it may be a joke, it's likely to be true that many of your ancestors traveled by ship to their new country. Ships of all types left various regions around the globe with the United States as their destination. Your living relatives may even know what the name of the ship was because of family stories.

The best way for you to learn about your ancestors is through public records and oral histories. Once you have done your best to get your living relatives to tell you everything that they know, you now need to use public records. What public records are available to help you learn how your ancestors arrived in North America? There are actually many ways.

One method that can be helpful to some is that of ship passenger lists. If you can learn about what time and what city your family came in at, you may be able to find information about the ship that brought them, which means you could get your hands on passenger lists, if they have been kept.

These can help you to learn more about who came with your family to the country, when they arrived and any deviations from names.

Next, use immigration paperwork to help you. This information is ideal for those that are looking for information regarding who their family members came here with, when they arrived, how they arrived, as well as where they went when they came here. Immigration paperwork is usually something that people keep, but if not there are public records that can additional help with it. The best place to find it would be through the location that they came in from.

In addition, many people came to the United States and then received naturalization paperwork. This paperwork is generally kept somewhere safe, but if not, again, it is public record information. In this case, though, naturalization paperwork and records would be available through the city or state in which they were naturalized. This is generally where they lived at that time.

Then Where Did They Go?

Once people arrived in the United States, or neighboring countries, they didn't necessarily stay in that location. Many traveled to locations where other family members where located or where they heard there would be jobs. Traveling was very common for those the immigrated into the country and it can be something difficult for you to trace.

Nevertheless, you need to do your best to do just that. Many people were able to purchase property, which means that you can use public records of property records to help you to find them. Other public record searches can help too. Learning this information is key to finding your family's history.

Genealogical Information And Tools To Use

Now that we've talked a great deal about the ways that you can find information about your family members, you may be wondering how you can do just that. After all, information isn't going to just come to you by visiting or contacting those locations.

There are actually a number of methods that you can use to track your family's history and your family tree. Let's go through several methods that are key to helping you to learn about your family.

Types of Genealogical Information

There are several key pieces of information necessary to use during your search. This includes information such as family names, occupations, place names, and dates.

Family Names

Family names are some of the most important pieces of information available to you. A family name is a name that's passed down from generation to generation as a link.

As a researcher trying to find out more about your family, it's key information that you need. Yet, family names can become quite confusing. Technically, your family name, or surname, is the name that is used to determine which family you belong to. In addition, in the English language it's the last name. But, in other cultures, that's not the case. It can be the name that comes first, such as in the Chinese culture's methods.

One of the largest problems with family names is just how often they change. Spellings often change, especially when you go back into centuries ago. When this happens, the only way to really find the connection is to realize the phonetic spelling of the name now and then.

This is important for one reason: public records may be in any variation of the name and therefore to keep your search going, you need to have this information.

In fact, one of the largest problems you may encounter is the name changes that happened when individuals came into the country during the large surges throughout the centuries. Names often were said by immigrants to those admitting them. They were spelled the way that they sounded.

In addition to this, family names have additional complications you'll need to deal with. For example, the family name may have been taken on by someone as they were married, or by their step parent. If they were adopted or if they were fostered, they could have had a name change.

Of course, when tracking the women in your family, you'll need to realize the difference between maiden names (prior to marriage) and their husband's surnames that they then took on.

Many times these name changes are located in some form of public record, but that's not always the case. Sometimes official records did not take hold. This can then be important for you to learn through oral histories.

In addition to this, if your family has a family name that is very common, such as Jones, then you may have an even harder time finding your ancestors. Even if your name is not all that common, though, you still shouldn't assume that anyone with your family's name is related to you, as that's not necessarily true.

Occupations

Occupations that your family members had may also be helpful to you for additional reasons. In fact, if two people have the same surname, their occupation may be able to differentiate the two people from each other.

In addition, occupational information can help you with learning political interests as well as social status for each person in the family. And, as was often the case, trades were often shared in the family. A father may have passed down his trade of glassmaking to his son.

When considering occupation, though, keep these things in mind.

- Census records were often embellished. People wanted to look better than they were.

- Jobs often changed from the beginning of their lives to later in their lives.

- Seasonal work often played a role, too.

- Names for the jobs that you know of them now may be different then.

- There are likely to be different terms for the same occupation. Various regions have their own terms for use in defining occupations.

To find out the occupational information of your family members, you can use census records, trade directories, vital records as well as professional organizations that they may have been a part of.

Place Names

The good and bad news is that place names are part of the process of finding your family. The good news is that these can reveal quite a bit of information. The bad news is that the names often change from language to language and over time, making it difficult for you to track.

In older cultures, names were always spelled differently in various public records and by scribes. Why is this? They weren't always as literate as they liked to think that they were. Plus, dialects and various other things could have changed them over time.

In addition to that, some locations around the globe have the same name, but are nowhere near each other. Or, these locations themselves could have changed. As borders changed, names of cities and regions also changed. In some cases, locations, certain villages, did no longer exist due to the dying out of residents through famines or disease.

Nevertheless, this information is very valuable to those that are looking for family histories. Therefore, you have to do your best to work through the process. To find information about the places that your family could have lived, start with the public records that we've listed above. Vital records, deeds, census information, as well as taxes can all be used to track this information.

You can also find out a lot about how the locations have changed through a brief history lesson on the region. You can learn much of this through encyclopedias or online resources. It could prove to be vitally important.

Dates

Another need for information comes from dates. But, here you want to be very cautious as even oral histories regarding dates can be misunderstood or information could have been passed down incorrectly. Indeed it is common for some information to be purposefully misrepresented. For example, someone may lessen their age so that they could join the military.

Another common error is that which is made to cover up a pre-marriage pregnancy, in which the child's birth information is altered or marriage dates are changed to reflect this information.

As you go back in time, you should take note of calendar changes that were also in place. For example, the first of the year has changed often from one date to the next. The movement to the Gregorian calendar from the Julian calendar can be a potential problem causer, too.

One key factor to remember is that when you are using dates to track information, those dates that are recorded close to the event are often the most accurate. The birth of a child is more accurate on its birth certificate because this is often filed right away. Family Bibles are also an ideal tool.

As you go through your search, you may also need to consider other pieces of information to gather the information that you need.

There is no one way to make sure you learn all that you can about your family tree. The fact is you need to take into consideration whatever is out there and then completely investigate it.

Reliability

A very important factor in the process of searching for any of these things is the reliability of the source. There are countless things that could make this difficult. Yet, as a researcher, you need to take into account the probability that information is accurate, or not.

This means taking into account the method that the information was obtained, the state of mind that it was given as well as what can support it. Reliable or not, it may still be a tool that helps you piece together your family's story.

Getting Help

There is nothing wrong with getting some help for your family tree and history search. In fact, if you want to go back deep into time, you really should consider getting some professional help.

Since most genealogical studies will start with the present and work back as much as possible, it's sometimes inevitable that you'll hit a dead end. Unless you are a professional and know how to analyze information for clues regarding the next leap (or simple know how to leap) then you may just not be able to go any further.

There are several ways that you can get help. Here, we'll briefly talk about the methods that can help your search as well as how to choose them.

Hiring a Professional

Probably the most expensive option for you to use is that of hiring a professional genealogist. These individuals are likely to provide you with the highest quality results, if you select one that is responsible, experienced and dedicated to providing the information to you.

Hiring a professional to do this work for you is a good idea, especially if you find yourself at a road block. Yet, it is essential that you do your homework to find someone that is willing and capable of providing you with the information that you need. There are, unfortunately, many organizations that are only looking for a payday rather than looking to help you to put together your family's story.

Find out what history that professional offers. What has he done for others? What is the farthest back he or she has been able to go for other families? In addition to this, you want to know how it will happen. Where will they gather additional information, how will they do more than you did and what can you expect to learn from what you are offering them?

In getting this information, you should also make sure that the professional will be providing you with an accurate family tree. For example, it makes no benefit to you to be filled with inaccurate information, and since you likely have no way of knowing if it's authentic, you need an upfront guarantee.

Getting references for those that you employ and then understanding what they really can offer you is essential. Make sure to check them out with the Better Business Bureau or similar organizations as well.

Family Tree Software

There are two types of genealogical software that you can purchase. By far the best is that which will help you to store, organize and later display the family tree information that you determine. This type of software is a benefit especially when a paper like tree would be too much to keep organized.

The other type of software available is that which can help you to find your family tree members. Some of this family tree software is only basic in what it can offer, some are much more thorough. Although not nearly as beneficial as using a professional genealogist, this software can help to point you in the right direction and help you to fill your tree in.

When selecting software for your use with your family tree project, realize that not all software is the same in quality. One of the best things you can do is to look for reviews of specific programs from the web and from other consumers that have used it. This will give you the best estimate of the quality and the worth of the software to you.

Using additional resources for your family tree search is important to those that want to go as far as they can with their search. Not only will it help to do this, but these tools can make organizing and time management of this large project much easier on you.

Finding Information Online

There are many online websites that will give you access to all sorts of records, including social security records. Ancestry.com is one of the sites that do just this. The problem with using this site is that you sign up for a monthly or yearly fee and then may forget to cancel it. You have to keep track of how long you are on the site and when you are finished, be sure to cancel, unless you plan on using this site for more information.

They have access to all sorts of records, not just social security records. In addition to social security records, which are a great help, they have access to the following:

- Birth records
- Death certificates
- Military records
- Immigration records
- Marriage certificates
- Social security information

Yes, you can get all this information for free - it is all of public record and available to the public who wants to look for it. But this site cuts to the chase and saves you an inordinate amount of time in finding the information that you are looking for.

Instead of spending weeks to get records from social security, you can get it in a matter of seconds when you use an online website. While you have to pay a fee for the online records, you still have to pay a fee to get anything copied at the county recorder's office or social security office.

While social security is your first step, it is only one of many. Social security records will tell you when a person was born and when they died, as well as the county in which they last lived. That's it. Finding your long lost relatives is like putting together the pieces of a puzzle. You have to go from record to another in obtaining information. So, yes, theoretically, you can find out information through the regular channels without having to pay a fee for the use of an online website, but it will take you a long time. If you want to find out the information quicker, you should use an online site.

When you are using an online site, you are not limited to social security records or any one particular record. You can get other information. You can even share the information that you get with other family members who may be looking for the same information as you. By joining an online website to look up your family members, you can find family members that are long lost to you but are still alive, and seeking out answers the same way that you are. You can share information with them and they can also share it with you. It makes getting information easier.

Another online site that you can use to get information about your relatives is none other than Facebook. Through this site, which was originally exclusively for college students who were too grown up to use MySpace, you could find out all sorts of information from distant relatives, who you can meet through this site. You can share information and photos at the touch of a button.

You should leave no stone unturned when you are seeking out information. Facebook is a good way to connect with living relatives who may be able to provide you with leads on where you want to go.

In addition to finding out this information for yourself, you should also think of your descendants who may one day ask questions about their ancestors. This is a nice gift that you can give to your children and grandchildren. Young people are not so much interested in this type of family history, but are very likely to be so as they get older.

The internet is a powerful tool for finding out information. And it is an excellent tool for searching for ancestors and long lost relatives. Online websites have not only helped hundreds of thousands of people connect with those with whom they have lost touch over the years, but they have also been able to answer burning questions that many have had about their own relatives.

Joining an online website is a good idea if you want to get some answers fast. There are many sites online that can provide you with ancestry information. Take a look at what the site provides by way of records, make sure that there are no extra fees for getting some records (some sites will give you a free sampling of the social security records as these are so easy to obtain but then charge for additional records) and then make sure that you can get a site that will give you unlimited access to all records for one fee.

It may seem to be costly to spend one fee for access to all records, but in the long run, if you are serious about finding out information about your ancestors, it will be the best option. As you continue to find out records and information, you will become increasingly reliant on the site. If you have to pay for each piece of information that you obtain, you will end up paying a lot more than a membership fee to the site.

Take a look around and see which sites are out there to accommodate you. Make sure that they have a good rating when it comes to reviews. For example, I have checked out social security records (free) on Ancestry.com as well as other sites. I found that not all sites are created equal. Some of them did not have these basic records. You want to be sure that the site that you use is one that is accurate and up to date with all records.

You may think that using a cut rate site is the way to go, but chances are that you are going to end up with a lot of dead ends. You are better off to investigate the sites that are out there and go with one that you can trust.

Online relatives lookup is the best way that you can find long lost relatives and create a family history. Be sure to also take advantage of free sites like Facebook to find living relatives who can provide you with a clue to where you want to head. Also, remember to look for the facts concerning your relatives and do not just go by stories and rumors that other people have been handing down from generation to generation.

Getting Others in on the Act

It is important that you get others in on the act when you are searching for your family members.

The more people you get involved in your search, the better off you are. They may have pictures of relatives that you do not have. They may have stories to share or information to give. They may be able to clear up misconceptions that you have about your relatives. They are your distant relations and part of your family history, too.

You can join several sites, if you so choose, to connect with long lost relatives. Many of these sites charge an annual fee to belong, but sites like Facebook are free.

Not only will you get more information when you join in with others when you are researching family history, but you will also get to connect with relatives that you never even knew existed in this manner.

Conclusion

You now have a good idea of where you family tree project needs to go. You can see that you need to start with the basics, no matter how basic they need to be. Then, go back in time, step by step, generation by generation, creating branches for your family tree.

It is likely that you will come to road blocks. And, you may stumble upon many different road blocks along the way. If you are to be successful, though, it means coming back to the process over and over again to analyze your next move. In some cases, you may even have to deal with family members that don't want to help or perhaps have a dark secret they aren't willing to share even if it will help your project.

Yet, a family tree leads to a full understanding of where your family came from. It is said that all people are related to a certain level. Someplace, many centuries ago, there was a connection to all of those on Earth. Yet, you won't be able to get that far back. You will be able to get through the process enough to find the answers to questions that you have.

Even better, you'll be able to see your family in a much clearer manner. Many times, family tree projects lead to understanding about decisions, about secrets and even about the people that you love. These projects are often well worth the time investment that they present.

You may think that family history is something that goes back in time. But you are actually living your own family history right now. Your children are the product of history. One day, their descendants will wonder about you. It is important to keep records and memories so that they can be passed down from one generation to the next.

You can do this by keeping scrapbooks, bits of information and giving your children and grandchildren as much information as possible about your own family. While my own kids, who are teenagers, are not much interested in their ancestors, I trust that one day, like me, they will be. This is why the information that I get from searching for family history is not only important for me, but also important for my children. I want them to be able to make it easy for them to be able to at least trace my roots when they get older and know who their relatives are.

You can keep the information online as well as in scrapbooks. Make copies as so many records can be lost. If you use an online site, you can easily create a family tree. You can put in as much information as you can into the family tree so that your children and their children will not have to wonder about you.

By researching your family history, you are doing much more than just finding out your own roots. You are building your own family history for your children, grandchildren, great grandchildren and your descendants.

Someday, you will be the person who someone will want to know about. Have fun finding your own family history, but be mindful of the fact that as you live, you are also making your own family legacy.

Resources

National Records Websites

www.archives.gov/genealogy
www.socialsercurity.gov
www.va.gov

Church of Latter-Day Saints Website

www.familysearch.org

Genealogy Websites

www.ancestry.com
www.genealogy.com
www.rootsweb.com
www.worldvitalrecords.com

Association of Professional Genealogists

www.apgen.org

Family Tree Software

www.familytreemaker.com
www.legacyfamilytree.com
www.rootsmagic.com

Website Database

www.cyndislist.com

Social Networking Websites

www.facebook.com
www.myspace.com

Molecular Genealogy Research Project

www.smgf.org

The Genographic Project

https://genographic.nationalgeographic.com